Hard Work

Sarah Fleming

OXFORD
UNIVERSITY PRESS

OXFORD
UNIVERSITY PRESS

Great Clarendon Street, Oxford OX2 6DP

Oxford University Press is a department of the University of Oxford.
It furthers the University's objective of excellence in research, scholarship,
and education by publishing worldwide in

Oxford   New York

Auckland   Cape Town   Dar es Salaam   Hong Kong   Karachi
Kuala Lumpur   Madrid   Melbourne   Mexico City   Nairobi
New Delhi   Shanghai   Taipei   Toronto

With offices in

Argentina   Austria   Brazil   Chile   Czech Republic   France   Greece
Guatemala   Hungary   Italy   Japan   Poland   Portugal   Singapore
South Korea   Switzerland   Thailand   Turkey   Ukraine   Vietnam

Oxford is a registered trade mark of Oxford University Press
in the UK and in certain other countries

British Library Cataloguing in Publication Data

Data available

ISBN 978-0-19-919872-6

17 19 20 18 16

Printed in China by Imago

Acknowledgements

The publisher would like to thank the following for permission to
reproduce photographs: **p4**t Bubbles Photo Library, b Sylvia Cordaiy/John
Parker; **p5** Mary Evans Picture Library; **p7** Ronald Grant Picture Library; **p8**
Illustrated London News; **p12** Billie Love Historical collection; **p13** National
Museums of Scotland Picture Library; **p14**t Topham Picturepoint, b Billie
Love Historical Collection; **p17** Billie Love Historical Collection; **p22**t Billie
Love Historical Collection, b and inset New Lanark Conservation Trust; **p23**
Mary Evans Picture Library; **p25** Billie Love Historical Collection; **p31** Billie
Love Historical Collection

Cover photograph by Topham Picturepoint

Illustrations by Leo Broadley: **p26/27**; Alice Englander: **p6**, **p8**, **p9**, **p10**, **p11**,
p13, **p15**, **p18**, **p19**, **p20**, **p24**, **p28**, **p29**, **p30**; Janek Matysiak: **p3**, **p16**

Contents

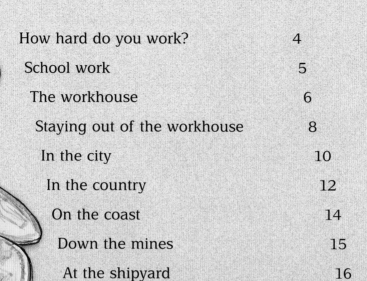

How hard do you work?   4

School work   5

The workhouse   6

Staying out of the workhouse   8

In the city   10

In the country   12

On the coast   14

Down the mines   15

At the shipyard   16

At the mill   17

The government investigates   19

Improvements for working children   21

Illness and injury   23

Street children   26

The flowergirl's story   28

The thankless job   31

Glossary and sources   32

In Victorian money
12 pennies (12d) = 1 shilling (1s or 1/-).

In 1880, 1 penny bought a small penny
loaf (of bread) or a stamp.

How hard do *you* work?

Do you:

◆ make your own bed?
◆ have weekly chores to do?
◆ get paid for doing them?

Child work laws in the UK today

Children under the age of 13 are not allowed to work unless they have a special license, e.g. for modelling.

Children between the ages of 14–16 can do light work for up to two hours a day after school and on Sundays, and five hours on Saturdays.

In most countries today there are laws to stop people employing children in hard jobs or for long hours. But in 2002, 211 million children aged 5–14 worldwide worked full time. Children have to work hardest where people are poor and don't have any education.

We understand today that children need time to play and time to learn. But in the Victorian times, that understanding was just beginning. This book looks at the hard lives of poor children in the United Kingdom in the 19th century.

School work

Free, compulsory education for 5–13 year olds was not available until the 1890s. Before that, education was patchy. Most schools cost money – the amount depended on the type of school.

Some children went to schools which were more like baby-sitting; some went to schools where they were made to work. Most children didn't go to school for very long and worked before or after school. Many didn't go to school at all.

The workhouse

The workhouse – or the poorhouse – was the lowest of the low. If you couldn't pay your bills you were sent there. But it was so horrible that people preferred to live in the grottiest hovels and do the most disgusting jobs than to be sent there.

Why were they so bad? Local councils had to have workhouses for the poor. But they didn't want to have to pay to look after poor people. So they made the workhouses as nasty as possible so only the really desperate would go to them.

Life in the workhouse

- When you arrived you were separated from your family.
- You had to obey lots of rules, and if you didn't you were punished.
- There was little food: gruel, a watery porridge soup, and bread were the main diet.
- You had to work hard. Breaking up stones to make gravel for roads was one job; picking fibres from old ropes (**oakum**) was another.

Workhouses in the early part of the 19th century used to 'sell' their children to people as **apprentice** workers. These children were often kept in locked dormitories at night so that they wouldn't escape.

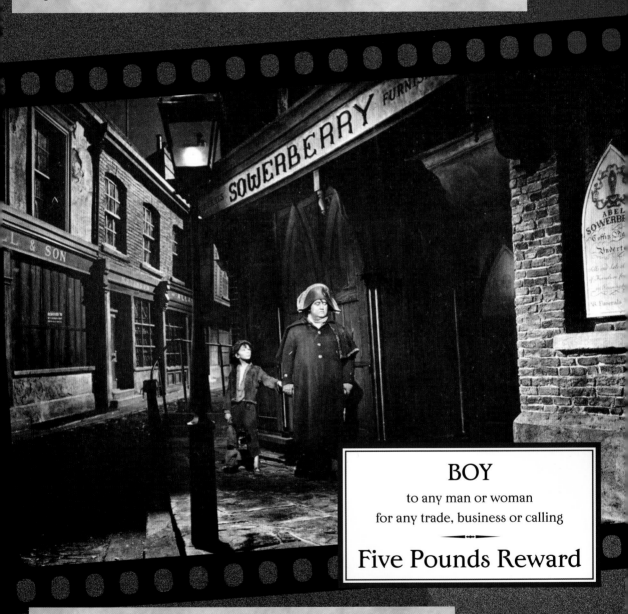

BOY

to any man or woman
for any trade, business or calling

Five Pounds Reward

In *Oliver Twist* by Charles Dickens, Oliver (9) is made to pick oakum at the workhouse. Then he is given to an **undertaker** who is paid five pounds to take him away.

Staying out of the workhouse

In 1847 this family just escaped the workhouse. The whole family worked at home making wooden toys.

The father did the heavy work, cutting and preparing large pieces of wood. But he got very sick and couldn't work. To keep the family from the workhouse his 15-year-old daughter took on his work – the work of a strong grown man. She told Henry Mayhew:

"I alone could save him from the workhouse. I never feel tired over it, because I know that it is to make him comfortable"

Henry Mayhew wrote about the poor in a London newspaper. His writing helped to improve and change laws about the poor and working conditions. He rarely named the people he interviewed.

The toymaker became bedridden but began to do light work again. He told how the family also made mousetraps.

"The four of us can make twenty-four dozen of the traps in a day... we can earn about a penny an hour..."

"I make the springs, cut the wires, and put them in the traps. My daughter cuts the wood, and makes the doors... My wife nails the frames... and my son pulls the wires into the places after I have entered them. Then the wife springs them, after which the daughter puts in the doors, and so completes them." [1]

In the city

Fur-pulling

Women and girls were employed to pull the fur off dead animals.
The fur was used as stuffing and the skins to make coats.
A Victorian writer wrote:

If you had ever seen a room
crowded with girls pulling the fluff from cats,
rabbits, rats, and goodness knows what other animals,
you would appreciate the situation better. The fluff, the
down, and the small hairs smother everything, and are
necessarily swallowed by the occupants of the room with
disastrous effect. Yet some of the men in the trade force their
employees to eat under such circumstances, that is, to
swallow their food thickly coated with the hairs from
which nothing can preserve it.

Why do not
the women refuse? Because if they
did they would lose their jobs. There are
always hundreds ready and eager to
take their places. [2]

Mudlarking

The name 'mudlarking' makes this job sound like fun, but it wasn't. At low tides, children looked for things to sell in the cold, sludgy mud by rivers flowing through big cities. Old nails, bits of coal – even a length of rope might fetch a halfpenny.

Smelly jobs

If you could bear it, you could climb down into the sewers and see what valuables might have been lost down there. Or you could offer to take people's rubbish away and look through it in the hope of finding something worth keeping or selling.

In the country

You got paid for some jobs in the country, you did others to help out your family. There were jobs from picking up cow pats (which were used as **fertilizer**) to haymaking.

Children sowing potatoes.

Some jobs were seasonal. In spring you might have to strip bark (used to tan leather). In summer you might scare birds off the crops. At harvest time children were sent to do the gleaning: picking up any ears of corn left in the fields. Potato picking in autumn was back-breaking work.

Bringing home firewood.

Hired help

Janet Bathgate, a shepherd's daughter was hired out by her family at the age of seven for a small wage and her keep. Her jobs included herding the cow, fetching peat for the fire, milking the lambs, cleaning out the barns, digging potatoes, sweeping the house and washing up.

Out all day in the field could be boring.

ఞ13ఞ

On the coast

At low tide, children gathered shellfish, worms (for fish bait) and seaweed (for fertilizer) to sell.

Herring girls

Girls worked at fishing ports, **gutting** fish. Huge shoals of herring used to migrate down the North Sea every summer. A fishing fleet went with them, and 'herring girls' went too.

Up to 2,000 girls and women started work in the Shetlands in May. Working wherever the catch came in, they followed the fleet over the summer down the east coast of Britain to Norfolk.

They lived in over-crowded huts that reeked of fish and they got covered in fish scales.

Down the mines

In 1842, a 12-year-old girl told about her life as a coal bearer. She carried about 60 kilograms of coal up from the coal face (which could be anywhere between 180–450 metres below the ground). She did this 25–30 times a day. That's like climbing Ben Nevis (1344 metres) every day with a grown-up on your back!

"I am frequently in water up to the calves of my legs. When I first went down I fell frequently asleep while waiting for coal from heat and fatigue. I do not like the work, nor do the lassies (girls), but they are made to like it. When the weather is warm there is difficulty in breathing, and frequently the lights go out." 3

At the shipyard

Isambard Kingdom Brunel's huge ship, the *SS Great Eastern*, was built with twin hulls. The inner hull was made first, and then the outer one.

While the outer one was being made, riveters and their 'bashboys' had to spend whole days and sometimes weeks in the tiny space – only 0.8 m wide – between the hulls. Their only light was a candle.

Legend says that when the *SS Great Eastern* was broken up in 1888, because it was no longer used, the body of a man and a boy – riveters who had been trapped – were found between the hulls!

At the mill

Mills were very dusty because of the fluff that came off the cotton, and they were kept very hot – almost 30° Celsius – to make it easier to spin the cotton.

Why employ children?

They're small, so:

◆ they can squeeze between and under moving machines, cleaning them and changing bobbins;
◆ you need less space between the machines, so more machines fit into a room;
◆ you can pay them less, and punish them more than adults.

Time keeping and punishment

This boy worked 14 hours a day at a Dundee spinning mill. Even with these long hours he says that the managers used to put the clocks back to make them work longer.

Once, he was looking after a machine which was running too fast and he couldn't keep up with his job so his boss shouted at him.

"I told him I was doing the best I could. He flew into a furious passion…and lashed me cruelly. He then seized me by the ears and hung me for a few moments over a window three storeys from the ground." [4]

The government investigates

Some people were worried about children working so hard. The government set up **committees** to report on conditions in factories. A committee **chairman** asked children, parents and bosses to describe their lives. Here are some extracts:

The child – sold by the workhouse as an apprentice

Robert Blincoe: When I was four I… went to St Pancras workhouse… when I was six or near seven I was made over to the owners of a mill near Nottingham.
Chairman: Were you ill-treated?
Robert: Oh, I have scars still to prove it.

The boss – hours of work

Chairman: What were the hours of work?

John Moss: I always got them up at half past four to get them ready for the mill, and they were always to be at the mill by five o'clock, winter and summer and never later.

Chairman: Did the children sit or stand to work?

John Moss: Stand.

Chairman: The whole of their time? Were there any seats in the mill?

John Moss: None.

Chairman: Were they very much fatigued?

John Moss: Yes, there were always some of them missing every night – I have found them asleep on the mill floor. [5]

Improvements for working chidren

The reports from the committees, and the writings of people like Henry Mayhew, helped to make the government bring in new laws.

Gradually, over the 19th century children were:

◆ made to work fewer and fewer hours, e.g.
   1847: mill children down to 10 hours a day;
◆ 1880: factory children down to half a day;
◆ taken out of the work force, e.g.
   1844: no under 8s in mills
   1891: no under 10s in any industry.

By 1891 there was compulsory education for all children under 10.

The laws helped

	1851	1871	1901	1911
Boys	36.6%	32.1%	21.9%	18.3%
Girls	19.9%	20.5%	12.0%	10.4%

This table shows the percentage of children in England and Wales aged 10–14 at work. The numbers are taken from **censuses** – forms that the government makes people fill in every 10 years to find out about the population of the country.

The table shows that the number of children aged 10–14 who did paid work became fewer as new laws were introduced. But the figures don't show the whole story. People may not have been honest. They may not have told the government about unpaid or **casual work** that children did, or work that the family did as a whole (like the toymakers on pages 8 and 9) in case they had to pay tax on this.

Not all factory owners were bad. Some made their workers feel as though they belonged and were valued. In the *Rowntrees* chocolate factory in York, for example, there was a library for workers to use, and workers under 17 were given free education.

Rowntrees Factory Library

Robert Owen

Owen had worked in the mills himself as a boy. When he became a mill owner he wanted to make life easier for his workers.

- ◆ He cut down the working day for children.
- ◆ He built a school in the village.
- ◆ He tried to make parliament make new laws to improve children's working life.

New Lanark Mill

Illness and injury

In the 19th century people didn't think about health and safety at work. This was partly because Victorians didn't understand about some illnesses, and partly because bosses didn't care about their workers.

Cancer

Chimney sweeps got a special kind of cancer (and lung disease too) from breathing in coal dust. They often had to sleep in cellars on bags of coal dust, with nowhere to wash. Some chimney sweeps suffocated to death by breathing in the coal dust when they were cleaning the chimneys.

THE LONDON SWEEP.

[From a Photograph.]

Mind your fingers!

Read this account written by a journalist in 1883:

If you were to give a tea-party to saw-mill boys, the thing that would astonish you would be the difficulty of finding half a dozen of your guests with the proper number of fingers.

I know one little lad who is employed at pulling out the planks which have been pushed through the machine by men, and he has one hand now on which only the thumb is left. [6]

Deformed back

Elizabeth Bently: I was middling strong when I went to the mill, but I got bad health… I pulled my bones out of place.

Chairman: You dragged baskets?

EB: Yes… A great basket that stood higher than this table… And pulling it pulled my shoulder out of its place and my ribs have grown over it.

Chairman: You are deformed?

EB: Yes, I am. I was about thirteen years old when it began and it has got worse since. Before I worked in a mill I was as straight a little girl as ever went up and down to work.

(The witness was so overcome with tears that she was unable to continue.) [7]

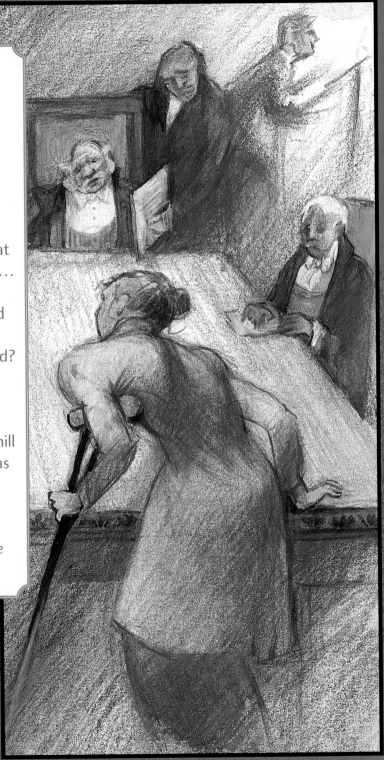

Phossy jaw

The tips of matches were made of white phosphorus. This attacked the lower jaws of people working in match factories. The illness began with toothache and swollen gums. In time the jawbone would rot away, and the area would glow greenish-white in the dark. If you weren't operated on you would die.

The only cure for phossy jaw was to cut out the jaw. Today, we use red phosphorus in matches, which doesn't cause this disease.

Street children

Begging

People from all over the world came to London. This family is selling religious papers.

'Finding' was a job too!

Costermongers sold fruit and vegetables.

While some children went into factories, and others worked with their parents at home, many earned a few pennies by working on the streets. Some were 'employed' and had specific jobs to do like selling toys or food. Others hoped to earn the odd penny by running errands, calling cabs for people, sweeping roads or picking up horse or dog dirt. Others became street performers, while some turned to crime…

Selling food

Pickpocket

About 41,000 birds were sold every year on London streets. The birds were caught in the country. Some sang, some were painted to look pretty.

Street performers

The flowergirl's story

This is the life of a young Irish flower seller, living and working in London in 1851. She rented a room in a house, and looked after her 11-year-old sister, who also sold flowers and her brother, who was a costermonger.

"I sell flowers, sir... so does my sister, all kinds ... primroses, violets, wallflowers, and roses. Gentlemen are our best customers. I've heard they buy flowers to give to the ladies."

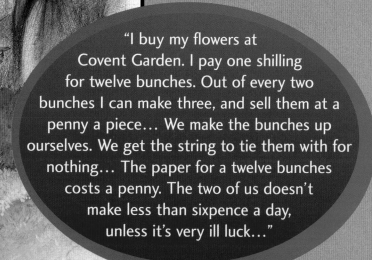

"I buy my flowers at Covent Garden. I pay one shilling for twelve bunches. Out of every two bunches I can make three, and sell them at a penny a piece… We make the bunches up ourselves. We get the string to tie them with for nothing… The paper for a twelve bunches costs a penny. The two of us doesn't make less than sixpence a day, unless it's very ill luck…"

	Money	
	Out	In
Buy 12 bunches for (1s = 12d) at Covent Garden	12d	
Make three bunches from every two	0	
String costs nothing	0	
Paper for a dozen bunches costs 1d , so for 18 bunches it costs $1\frac{1}{2}$d	$1\frac{1}{2}$d	
Sell for 1d a bunch		18d
Total out $13\frac{1}{2}$d	Total in 18d

$$Profit = 4\frac{1}{2}d$$

☞ Look back on page 3 to see what you can buy with a penny.

"Mother died seven years ago last Guy Fawkes Day. I've got myself, and my brother and sister a bit of bread ever since, and never had any help but from the neighbours… We can all read… I put myself, and I put my brother and sister through Ragged School."

"If it's bad weather, so bad that we can't sell flowers at all … the landlady lends us one shilling … We live on bread and tea, and sometimes a fresh herring of a night. Sometimes we don't eat a bit all day when we're out; sometimes we take a bit of bread with us, or buy a bit." [8]

The thankless job

The average family in Victorian times had six children, and having thirteen was not unusual. Older children were often expected to look after the younger ones.

It often happens that a mere baby of six or seven years old will have to lug about a great infant, which is altogether beyond her strength; while at the mature age of eight years many a poor hungry-eyed, wistful little creature has the care of an entire family, proceeding in regular gradations from the boy only a year younger than herself, to the staring-eyed little stranger of a few weeks old, which is destined to be nursed on door-steps, and to be comforted with moist sugar tied up in a bit of rag, while it is cutting its teeth by the aid of the ring of a street-door key. [9]

So, the next time you are made to tidy your room and you think that's hard work – think again!

Glossary

apprentice – a person who serves their employer and is taught a trade

bobbins – cotton reels on sewing machines

casual work – work that comes up by chance or irregularly, and there is no record of the worker being paid

census – form that the government makes people fill in every ten years to find out about the population of the country

chairman – a person in charge of a committee

committee – a number of people who are asked to investigate or manage something

fertilizer – something put on the soil to enrich it

gutting – removing the 'guts' and insides from fish

oakum – the fibres of old ropes sold to ship builders, mixed with tar, and used to seal the lining of wooden ships

riveters – a person who fits rivets – heated metal plugs put into holes in two sheets of metal. As the rivet cools it draws the metal sheets together.

undertaker – someone who arranges funerals

Sources
(footnoted numbers):

1 Henry Mayhew: letters to the *London Chronicle*. This letter is reproduced on the internet at http://www.victorianlondon.org/mayhew/mayhew37.htm. The same website has many other letters by Mayhew.

2 From *How the Poor Live*, George Sims, 1883.

3 Extract from Royal Commission Reports, 1842 on *The Employment of Children and Young Persons in the Mines and Collieries*, quoted in *Working Children*, Derek Ogston and Margaret Carlaw, Ballieknowe Publishing, 2003.

4 Extract from Chapters in *The Life of a Dundee Factory Boy*, quoted in *Working Children*, Derek Ogston and Margaret Carlaw, Ballieknowe Publishing, 2003.

5 Extract from Royal Commission Reports, 1833 on *The Employment of Children and Young Persons in the Factories*, quoted in *Society and Industry in the 19th Century 2: Factory Reform*, Keith Dawson and Peter Wall, Oxford University Press, 1968.

6 *From How the Poor Live*, George Sims, 1883.

7 Extract from Royal Commission Reports, 1833 on *The Employment of Children and Young Persons in the Factories*, quoted in *Society and Industry in the 19th Century 2: Factory Reform*, Keith Dawson and Peter Wall, Oxford University Press, 1968.

8 Henry Mayhew, quoted in *The Street Traders' Lot: London 1851*, Stanley Rubenstein, Sylvan Press, 1949.

9 From *The Terrible Sights of London*, Thomas Archer, 1870.